Little Boy Blue

Jamal Mehmood

Burning Eye

BurningEyeBooks
Never Knowingly
Mainstream

This edition published by Burning Eye Books 2016

www.burningeye.co.uk
@burningeyebooks

Burning Eye Books
15 West Hill, Portishead, BS20 6LG

ISBN 978-1-911570-05-9

For Mama and Abu

CONTENTS

WHAT IF THEY KNEW

nervous at the school gates
split fates and faces different
they ate rice with a fork
I with a spoon
my mother spoke her sweet punjabi
her sweet sweet punjabi
bended to every dialect
I stood by
itching to leave

what if they hear her
they'll remember I'm different
they'll ignore my face, won't they
they'll ignore her embroidery
they'll ignore her kameez
they'll ignore her shalwar
they'll ignore my name
while they say it so differently

mama and abu
clasping what they can
of what they left behind
those melodies and native tongue
on sunrise radio before school
I was itching to turn it down
close the door quickly
and turn my back on home

what if they heard where they come from
they'll ignore my ignorance
on pop culture references
they'll ignore my grandmother's broken english
sounding sweeter than a thousand sonnets in the queen's
if only I knew how sweet it was
I'd hold her hand a little tighter as she walked me home
where I'll always have to go

my grandfather scolds me in urdu
it burns twice
one for the scold
one for the urdu, one for the shame
I'm hoping he stops
they can't ignore that voice

what if they hear his journey
what if they hear the noble decision
what if they hear prison
what if they hear paris in the winter
what if they hear england spitting him out
what if they hear him swimming
what if they hear europe
what if they hear england saying come back
what if they hear him running

what if they hear the reason I'm here

FALLING STARS & CALLING CARDS (AN ODE TO GREEN STREET)

falling stars and calling cards
in this canvas of colour
just off the A2
a movable feast hemingway never graced
this is midnight in newham
I'll swap absinthe for lassi

she gives him a bite of her samosa because she loves him
and as his neck falls to take a bite
her eyes pull his to hers
to sounds of lyca radio silence
and for a moment the elation from this supernova
drowns out the fumes
from united halal meat

there's a paddy power
where kebabish used to be
I hope it stops here
because these food stores take us home
and our mother tongues
sound so beautiful in resonance
as she throws her dupatta
over trap drums and tabla

my sikh aunty sells meat to her muslim sister
this big-hearted society
remembers time before partition
and these storefronts give me hope
that all is not lost

KHALA, ROLL UP MY SLEEVES

roll up my sleeves again
so our palms cross paths
as they did
and when it's far enough
take my hand
and walk me into time memorial
far enough
till my hand grows smaller than yours
walk me past innocence
and please stay a while
remember to make me forget
painful reason that we left behind

towards moon river
just round the bend
show me all my friends
before I knew the differences

before skin knew deformity
born of pain
make it yesterday once more
yeah, those old songs
written before I knew
weighted words and wrongs
so intimately well

and take me just there, past calculation
that smelt of insanity and cold seclusion
before bold delusion
I hold confusion
in contempt
leave it in the bushes
of my old back garden
amongst the leaves
and forgotten tennis balls we couldn't find
some sunny day
where and when
we'd watch the races together
I'd support whoever you did

that this were blissful
would you not concur?
khala, roll up my sleeves
and take me to where we were

STARDUST MEMORIES

old photographs that belong to your grandmother
will tell you tales you never knew were penned
of small terraced homes
where small was enough
no proper sofa and bedsheets for makeshift curtains
and twenty-four-hour development at your local boots
son, you do not know what made you

some turn at the edges
a faint red date to remind you just how long it's been
these photos have habits of joy
before we all parted
and decided being together was all too much
before we all grew cold
and laid the blame on time
and began chasing something none of us can name
old photographs might remind you of your first step
make you question why you're always running
and the answer might tell you
that it runs in our family, child

they may hurt you to look
stop you in your tracks to wonder what changed
from stolen glances and imagination
to not a word between you two
and for a moment that silence is broken by memory
one you taught to subside
but these photographs don't listen
they've no mind of their own
they don't care for your half -healed heart
they just look back at you
eyes just as you remember them
you might learn why you haven't slept all these years
as the mess you made surrounds you
its grip only loosening to tell you
that death makes everything important

in these photographs sits everything worth having
the suit you wish you never wore
the songs your mother sang
and the one you still sing
when time tended not to move so quickly
and your destiny didn't seem so set in stone

what if you never find meaning?
any decent poet will tell you
to look within
but try some old photographs too
they could teach you that happiness was never milestones or superficial
but ice cream and a breeze
and a glance that still hasn't found a way out of your heart
and as you sit through tears from sepia
pulled from a decade lost
you'll realise that all your love was sleeping
beneath memories of stardust

SING ABOUT ME, I'M DYING OF THIRST

I'm a dying man
in a sea of similar souls
swimming well, resting
on your buoyancy

promise that you will
sing about me

write after loss
it might be therapy
sink with your ink
into my memory

if I leave myself and turn away
stepping toward eternity with only my own feet

promise that you will
sing about me

if my disposition differs
and withers into another form
if mellow sunsets deform into another dawn
if you even just begin to doubt me
just promise that you will
sing about me
promise that you will
sing without me

AN ODE TO THOSE WHO'VE MET BEFORE

way over yonder
and on street corners
close to our homes
you'll find penned reasons to hold me in contempt
even harm me
so in our sour times
friendship is counted twice
when held through screams of scorn
and bellowed bigotry
our silence speaks

it proves its worth
against the tales and poetry
how could it not?
with roots in love
there's proof enough
it was destined to succeed

oddities and rarities shared ordinarily
with a golden soul beneath golden suns
and our typical grey that plagues a little less
with solitary thought lent to another

this unfamiliar territory
chanced upon by a traveller
with a heart that warmed
through a spring that never came
and a summer that shone
and burned time past

laughter that would
light flames under january's snowflakes
and company that would
remain after parting
wither sorrow to ash
and turn me to gratitude
for fortunes upturned
in the mystery of patterns
spelled by God
that lie in paths trod
by those who've met before
called friends by some

HERE'S TO HOPING YOU CATCH SOME HEAVEN

I apologise
on behalf of them
those who chose to throw hell
into hands they forcibly thrust together
who broke in like a thief in the night
and took more than just your innocence
as if it wasn't enough
who broke bones, let alone your delicate hearts
who left you in the dark, the rain
attach
any connotation you wish
it'll fit
they were so terribly broad with their strikes
I apologise on their behalf
nonsensically
but let me
for each tear they wrenched out
for none to wipe away
in a sweet caress
for each infliction of horror
each hand they left dangling
each time they eroded your trust with the world
hacked away in rage or lust

I apologise
on their behalf
who put suicide in your thoughts
I dare not call them men
I can't tend to every hurt
every bruise
though my own hands
are here to be lent
joined together, at least
hoping you catch some heaven
after all
it's destined beneath your feet

A POEM FOR CYNTHIA ROSE

cynthia's dress
and hair she'd never touch
the oddest socks
go on cynthia!

let them with thoughts that don't part
partake privately in mutterings
break bread over
your paisley lunch box
and starfish and coffee
and whatever else
may take the fancy
of your pretty mind
that the colour-blind
could not even dream of
but only find laughter for

keep the secret notes in your lime-green notebook
poems to kindred strangers
that sit by sweet maple syrup
in that bag they all hate

your cares couldn't find time
to keep the callous
in your magic schedule of worthy causes
and earthly pauses
letting the light inside for a cup of tea
and a side order of ham

if they stay laughing so readily
go on cynthia
you're more beautiful
than they'll ever be

ON THE FAST TRAIN HOME

I read stories penned by cypriot hands
the man of african descent sits opposite
focused on our sorry state
laid bare in the evening standard

next to him she speaks a soft french
perhaps a name like mine
her skin a colour like mine
I think God used a touch more red

and next to me
another politely speaks
her face would be east of mine
on a map of where our great-grandmothers walked

another human reaches outer space on the front page
four scattered souls meet here on earth
one writes
one reads
one scrolls
one sleeps

it's a tiring world
but I'm glad we have each other
because even in our silence
there are latent stories
beneath gesture
and only necessary speech

I wonder
if our mothers are the same but different
if we share a gratitude for our fathers
I wonder if we spoke
would our hearts shed the weight of our days
if it would morph the monotony of survival
into life and laughter
if for those moments
our books would share a page
and our inks in all their colour
would paint us all in beauty and joy

I wonder what would happen
if we weren't so tired
if we weren't so lost
we could disappear in our tales
and meet mortality knowing something
other than ourselves

that there are others
others who live in mourning for the death of their childhood
others who wish they never awoke
who can't go back to sleep
and dream euphoria

others who walk this nightmare
wishing someone else would speak
and make a thousand pieces out of silence
a silence we can only remember
on the fast train home

WE

I am the grimace that meant no harm
the look of confusion misconstrued
hurried steps and heavy strolls
the ill-intentioned plaintiff
and vulnerable victim too

I am the flowing locks
that tie themselves
to tightened braids
I am coarse beauty
and ugly silk

I am open book
but closed mind
I am studious and spurious
luxurious and low
furious and slow

I am poverty-stricken
so a thief
no one struck me the blow
that thrust lack of love
into my shallow pockets

I stole a heart today

I am airtight's revenge
and the house that humility built
I set spirits alight
and burnt souls to the ground
and picked up ashes
and wrote art

after all was sung and painted
wasn't I beautiful?

HANDS

she drew moonglade with her fingers
painted stars only she could see
made a private peace with her small hands
while the world carried on
and I knew my hands had to do more
than build a lonely wealth
and hold up the powerful

what work is more noble
than to love in public
to use hands to lift
to hold hands, to take hands and shake hands
to share the burden of hands between hands
and unravel pain like a fist lost to soft peace

this must be done in plain sight
invisible hands make for ghost-like societies
and we are dying again and again
under the weight of hard hands
under the weight of the male ego
under the weight of hatred
and the hunger for a loving hand
a longing for a heaven free of callouses and coarse palms
somewhere to soak our bruised knuckles

and maybe a fountain of youth
is just nostalgia and a reminiscent moment
available for eternity
to those whose hands loved well enough

WAR ONCE MORE

we arrive again
at this tragic inevitability
our voices and our marches
rendered speechless once more

we are insulted

the invisible hand
of the great british bloodlust
covers our mouths
and applauds
and laughs
at our powerlessness
in this great democracy

we are insulted

the greatest purveyors of war
scurry forwards once more
returning to old lands
it seems eastern blood was drying
on their cursed hands
the hands that don't tire still
from asking others to kill

we are insulted

there are children
there are mothers bound to them
there are lovers
and beloveds bound to them
awaiting skies turning a harsher shade of fear
still longing for their setting sun

just look what you've done

RUNNING THROUGH THE COMMENTS SECTION WITH MY WOES

that is a reasonable viewpoint
that is hauntingly humbling
that is so terribly tragic
what could I do to help
how could anyone disagree
but wait, jamal
this is home of
they're taking over
this is we're full
this is monuments to racist heroes shouldn't fall
this is fear, this is war, this is us and this is them
this is assimilate or don't
because it really doesn't matter
this is pick and choose what we shouldn't forget
this is what we don't remember
this is what you should remember
this is 1066
this is 1918
this is 1945
this is 1966 and football's coming home

chelsea fans on a parisian train
this is we're racist we're racist and that's the way we like it
this is you fundraising on the high street and this is her saying don't
give it to them
this is for the floods in pakistan and this is him saying certainly not
this is your childhood hue falling in front of your young eyes
onto pages of your parents' tales coming true
this is the cold in england where we love to talk about the weather
and it is freezing now

more comments
stop scrolling, jamal
you'll grow up too fast
you'll grow up and hear your mum's voice on the phone a few
years later
telling you to be careful when you leave the library tonight
they smashed the window of your mosque
they made you feel this wasn't supposed to happen to you
they reminded you that this wasn't left in the eighties and decades
gone by

this was now
this is now
and I've done enough growing to know
that maybe ain't nothing changed but the weather
but that still means intermittent sunshine
so that still means we can try and move these clouds
that's a poor metaphor because you can't move clouds
I'm sure you know what I mean by now
so please excuse my soliloquy
I've just been running through the comments with my woes
and you know how that shit go

EVERYONE IS DEAD

the wars upon the land
had crawled ever closer
the distance from implosion
grew as thin as the skin
of those worn down
once tall, strong, historic

they had crawled ever so slowly
harsh claws
agony as they went
down the artist's throat
words fell upon brazen vocal cords
consumed by the hunger of war
his voice, fallen
like sweet angels forgotten

the wars they took his laughter's life
but his hands they knew not death
they played the strings
they sang his song
they wrote his passage
they became his lungs
they gave us gifts
his words too absent to give
so he played us poetry he dared not speak of
in quite so certain terms
so he played for us
the sounds of life
the haunt of war
that we might see
what we are dying for

everyone is dead
and no one knows anything
and the keys to the kingdom
lie with the monster
as he fights his savage
we are our brother's reaper
our mother's shame
and as for our sisters
there is only silence

THE DREAMS WE SELL OUR CHILDREN

daddy was an analyst
the boss was a masochist
the dreams we sell our children
are few and far between here
workplace nightmare
hurried steps – warfare
fees, universities, degrees
and epiphanies were mystery
and history was missing, we
left it in the past
for some new-age mimicry
corporation gimmicky
and everyone is him and me

make way for some well-adjusted denizen
engineering medicine
'cause anything is better than
shame
what's your name?
what do you do?
what is your occupation?
you mean how I live?
or how I make my living?

he said
what do you want to be when you're older
she said content
I don't want to be paid the same as a man
for a job we both resent
is this all you can offer
is it all you can present?
narrow options, no stock in my future
credit might default if I swap love for cash

so keep your broken pathways
I'll stay off the beaten track

A LETTER TO FUTURE SONS

weep, young man, weep
like your life depended on it

weep until you have craters
where tear ducts used to be
weep when you think of your mother
weep when you remember your father

your sisters have been weeping for an epoch now
weep so your sons can weep
so your daughters don't have to

Jesus wept
Muhammad wept
you are no messenger of God
so weep until the walls come falling down
boy, you have a soul beneath your skin
so weep and water the ground
where your fathers are buried
for not producing enough tears
and still producing you

so weep, young man, weep
I don't believe in your ornaments
your barriers are transparent
your lies lie in plain sight
I can see everything but tears

so weep, young man, weep
show me you live
show me you're more than I could ever be
show me nothing was in vain and I'm still alive

weep, young man, weep
for broken homes
for war zones
for tanks met with stones
weep for forgotten black faces
weep for body counts not on the tip of our tongues
weep for the songs we never sung
because we wouldn't cry
weep for the sky we couldn't see

and the forest we razed to the ground
weep for your ancestors
as you remember their names
and, my God, please weep for the children who weep too much
whose faces damned us to hell
as they told the story of our negligence
take your reticence
and crush it like we did your chances
under the malice of our hubris
and the inability of our eyes
to shed a single tear

so weep, young man, weep
put these pieces of man back together
deliver us from ourselves
and walk tall knowing tenderness is beautiful
and justice is love
and joy is peace
and so is success
so weep, young man, weep
like your life depended on it

because one day

it just might

EHSAN

chicken shop grease
paints his hands in a glow
neon signs and posters
a celebrity aura of the new kid at school
foreign tongue and a foster family
layers of a new world

his new white father finds the local mosque
and asks about bringing him often
so he doesn't lose touch

at school there is confrontation
slurs he has never heard
but knows what they mean
so it turns physical
he is left no choice
ehsan is no pushover
strength sits in him like a sleeping rock
he leaves them in awe

hit me, he says
to their surprise
knuckles to the cheek don't hurt like knowing he'll never go home
there were boots on his ground
so a knee to the stomach doesn't hurt like a mother that only exists
in memory
behind a glass exhibit titled
good things that happened a long time ago
and a father who can't feed him sweets at nowruz
no blow can hurt like that
so they hit and they hit and he stands tall
his blood knows to resist foreign forces
soon his reputation turns hard
and his fists become accustomed to being weaponised

he doesn't go to the mosque much anymore
except fridays where he sees boys whose lives mirror his own
he spends more time outside
finds the chicken shop welcoming
he's asked to work there and he wants the cash

now chicken shop grease paints his hands in a glow
he looks up
a woman in his mother's favourite colour kisses her son
and as her lips leave that blessed forehead
his hardened reputation is lost under the weight of what he's witnessed
he lowers himself behind the counter and drowns in the certainty of
never feeling his mother's embrace again
the stranger and her child hurry to his aid
what's wrong?
what's wrong?
his voice comes from the parting between the two parts of his severed
heart and he says

you look like mum

SOLITARY CONFINEMENT

these walls
made from smartphone glass
completely transparent so I cower in the corner
no power so I falter
spent hours in this torture
no rest for the sleeping, of course
the wicked are out in force
taking up space in your nightmares
and acres in your thoughts
hectares of tragedy in 140 characters
send me the link
let me corroborate the massacre
shed another tear and commentate upon the challenger
whisper another prayer and hope to God that this one manages
to help the heart of the person I've just seen cry
I couldn't see it coming down my eye
so I had to make the poem shed tears

the kingdom has come to this
britannia fears the waves
and won't remember what it did
blighty can't remember well
I can see it through the walls of the cell, I can't tell
whether this is just heightened information
or we're a blighted constellation
stars burning here on mother earth crying for help
I imagined what God thought of nuclear weapons
and the question answered itself
pain is streaming on these walls in 4k technicolour
if you see border patrol, immigration vans or britain first
warn a brother
the walls only get clearer
paying pittance to the cleaner
so I can see tweets for free
retweet for me

validate me with your retweet, baby
like me with your like
follow me with your love
remember me with your hashtag
all before you replace me
and watch another show from the grandstand
you hold panorama catastrophes
in the palm of your hand

MAYBE LUNGS WERE MADE TO FLOOD

maybe lungs were made to flood
and every road was meant to be walked
every sharp turn
was meant for more than just a curious stare
rivers were made not only for fish
but human arms and all our limbs
and weeping carried no shame
death carried no harm
in speech or in act
and living was never meant to be bare
feet were meant to kiss the earth
and stone and whatever else we thought of
had we lived
as we died

BACK HOME I

back home is mango and sugar cane residue
kaleidoscope memories
and your father's heart

it is roadside curation
making much from little
it is the perfect pronunciation of your name
it is tea in a glass
rice with your hands
and your mother's hope
that you don't forget
it is majesty and the moon
it is layla and majnun
the laymen know verses
we could only dream of writing

it is the bazaar and the darbaar
it is a favourable exchange rate
it is you haven't tasted better
don't eat from the street seller

back home is the sitar
the chaos of car horns
and a climate your blood remembers

BACK HOME II

but back home isn't yours
sons of those who destroyed it
return to find themselves
while you watch from afar
two flags
and a few words of two national anthems
one passport
and half an idea of what you're supposed to do

back home is not for you
your sheltered ways
your better days
your escapist's guilt

it is patience wearing thin
dark skin is still a sin
the colonial crumbs
it is breaking from within

back home may evade you
this island may evade you
this earth may evade you
but there is much peace to be made
in your lonely search

BOOGEYMAN

I sit at home and abroad
beautiful and unbound
touch my foreign skin
feed your appetite on my aura

watch my lips as they speak my truth
in all its red and exotic green
remembering my fearsome God
who, I state lucidly, is yours too

pine for my civilisation-building hands
read my poetry in secret corners
while you wish the words fell from your own heart

say my name in hushed tones
I am so low and lovely
my art is a type of kiss
they don't kiss where you come from

don't you just want our mouths to meet
again and again
you can't keep my flavours from your tongue
and your desire for my nakedness
is well documented indeed

aren't I the most beautiful boogeyman
you ever did see?

LITTLE BOY BLUE

fake trackies and hoody, you just wanna be accepted
hushed tones and closed mouths, you just wanna be accepted
always on the periphery, jamal, you just wanted to be accepted
sitting on the fence between sugar-coats and egg shells
you just wanted to be accepted
why?
maybe because when you were five a little girl told you
that people with brown faces weren't allowed at her party
maybe the news told her
there were terrorist jihadi paedophiles up in her midst
and nervous little paki boys who blow themselves to bits
but this was 1997
maybe she was a little pre-9/11 prophet
with right-leaning politics
or something far more normal
a daughter of her father that never changed
who made a little boy blue and just want to be accepted

no five-year-old deserves that confusion
but this is england
this is one-week summers in bradford and brixton
the equalities commission
and maybe I should change my name before application submission
and better shave your beard before your interview at cambridge just
listen

jab hamein yahan se nikalengein phir kahan jaogeh?

when they kick us out where are you gonna go?
I don't know
I can't wear a flag and be comfortable
the colours won't mix in the right shade
I can't conjure up the pride that my dad made
I'm learning
slowly

so, jamal, you can tell her now
that we're forcing entry to the party
we'll be late, and bring our own food
'cause egg and cress sandwiches
won't do for reparations

Thanks & Acknowledgements

Alhamdulillah.

Thank you to my grandfather for coming here and all he did. Thank you to my parents for all their love and sacrifice. My heart is full with gratitude and I know I can never repay you. Pray I do my best to.

To Ayyaz and Aroob. I love you both. Thank you for all the laughs.

To the small army of aunts who raised me. Mum, Nigi khala and Nuchi khala. To Maamoo for always being there and somehow always knowing what to do, and being a guide. To Nadeem, for all your time and help. Thank all of you for picking me up from nursery, school, university and the train station.

To my grandmother. Nano, you're the best and the veins of your old hands are my home. Windmill Road forever. Thank you to all my family for all the kindness and pride in me, including those sending love and prayers from Pakistan and every auntie and uncle who isn't related by blood.

To my fiancée Saffana. Thank you for always, always believing in me. For giving me courage, and for having the courage to love a poet. For being my best friend with a spirit like the sun.

To Aqeel and Nabeel, Haseeb. To Hussain and Hashem. To Adil and Akif. To our childhoods. To Qasim, Hassan and Hammad. To Mizan, Omar, Hashim and Zein. To Yusra, Sabah and Saira, Harleen, Za and Milandra. 87 USA forever. Poetic justice.

To Ankush, Anjalie, Ayo, Ashley and Allan. I'm blessed to have you. Thank you for all you've done and for being such solid friends.

To Rahima and Mabrur, thank you for keeping this kid under your caring wings for so long. To Rohima, for being there from when this poetry thing was getting started, for all the advice, belief, time and friendship. To Shakir, Eirteqa, Sana, Fori and Undleeb. To Zeenat (who gave me my first gig), Jahied, Marium, Irum Baji, Taz, Taslima, Nancy, Dil, Sayeda and the whole RB crew, all my love.

Thank you to Hassan Hirsi, for being so close from afar and having a soul made of magic.

To all the poets who have helped and encouraged me. To Zia, you're my favourite poet. I still can't believe I can text you. To Vanessa Kisuule, thank you for your time, your warmth and your help. And for gassing me up. To Zain Dada for always supporting me.

Thank you to Poetry Rivals, to Clive and Jenn at Burning Eye. To Sam, Samira and Media Diversified for supporting my work. To Nick Makoha for that workshop that made me realise I really wanted to do this. To all the poetry nights that let me on the microphone. To London.

Love to you all and anyone I missed. Khudaafiz.